This volume is produced with the assistance of the
Judge and Mrs Samuel D. Levy Memorial Publication Fund

Copyright © 1985 The New York Public Library, Astor, Lenox
and Tilden Foundations

Designed by Ronald Gordon & Dean Bornstein at The Oliphant Press

Distributed by the Publishing Center for Cultural Resources

Library of Congress Cataloging in Publication Data

Szladits, Lola L.
 Brothers : the origins of the Henry W. and Albert A. Berg collection of English and American literature, the New York Public Library.
 Bibliography: p.
 1. Berg, Albert Ashton, 1872–1950. 2. Berg, Henry W., 1858–1938. 3. Book collectors—United States—Biography. 4. Physicians—United States—Biography. 5. Book collecting—United States. 6. Berg Collection. 7. English literature—Library resources—New York (N.Y.) 8. American literature—Library resources—New York (N.Y.) I. New York Public Library. II. Title.
Z989.B455S94   1985   002'.075'0922 [B]   84–29605
ISBN 0-87104-281-9

Contents

Henry W. and Albert A. Berg:
I. Brothers, Physicians, New Yorkers 9

Albert A. Berg:
II. The Surgeon 17
III. The Collector 21
IV. The Trustee 33
V. The Man 39
References 47

Appendix A. Some Highlights of the Original Berg Collection 53

Appendix B. Documents of the Berg Gift and Bequest 57

Illustrations: following page 32

Henry W. and Albert A. Berg

*The past is a foreign country—
they do things differently there.*
L. P. Hartley
The Go-Between (1953)

I

Brothers, Physicians, New Yorkers

*Whatsoever thy hand findeth to do,
do it with thy might*—Ecclesiastes 9:10

Some unique personal qualities and a combination of fortunate circumstances went into the creation of one of America's great public collections of English and American literature. Two generations removed, facts can readily be distorted into a legend. It seemed appropriate, therefore, to re-examine the facts and to collect together what we know of a collecting pair of brothers.

Albert Ashton Berg, the youngest of eight children, was born in New York City on August 10 1872. There were three girls and five boys in the Berg family, of whom the oldest, Henry Woolfe, was born in 1858, in the "old country," what was then the Austro–Hungarian Empire. Their parents, Moritz Berg and Josephine Schiff, immigrated in 1862 to the United States, because his father could not provide for Moritz's medical training in Vienna, nor could Moritz himself support his own rapidly growing family.

Necessity made use of the skills he had hoped to use in surgery: Moritz Berg became a tailor in New York. Henry felt increasing responsibility to help his father support a large family. At the age of eleven, or so we are told, he got himself a job through the "Help Wanted" column as a page at the Cooper Institute (now Union) Library. Founded in 1839 by Peter Cooper "for the advancement of science and art," Cooper Institute offered free courses in science, engineering, electricity, and the liberal arts. The Institute also provided a reading room and library service.

Henry's love of books and learning was acquired early. While Peter Cooper was well known to the library staff, we know of a story that Henry was so conscientious in performing his duties as what was then known as "a checker," that he challenged the founder's identity when he wished admission to his own library. Mr Cooper was impressed by the security enforced by one so young. During a friendly conversation, Henry admitted his ambition to become a doctor and to fulfill the dream his father had cherished for himself. From then on, Henry looked forward to the visits of Mr Cooper, who, on one of those occasions, was accompanied by a heavily bearded man. Upon introducing the visitor as William Cullen Bryant, Henry recited a portion of "Thanatopsis," which naturally endeared him to the poet. The qualities apparent so early stayed with Henry for the rest of his life. He was devoted to members of his family, he was conscientious, and he remained an impassioned reader with a good memory.

Henry graduated from City College in 1878 as an honors student and received his medical degree from Columbia University's College of Physicians and Surgeons three years later. He specialized in the treatment of infectious diseases and was

Associate Attending Physician at Mount Sinai Hospital from 1898 to 1924 where he was also appointed physician for the isolation service. Henry served on the faculty of the College of Physicians and Surgeons, both as Assistant Professor of Neurology and Associate in Pediatrics, until his retirement in 1923. He also became widely known for his medical writings. Dr Henry Berg often appeared before congressional committees on economic matters and received thanks for his help in redrafting immigration laws.

It is not, however, for his career that the public remembers Henry Berg, but for his devotion to his youngest brother, Albert. Their father became critically ill in 1881, just when Henry had made arrangements to fulfill part of his dream: to go to the University of Vienna, then the pre-eminent medical school, to attend postgraduate studies. He cancelled his passage. After Moritz Berg died of cancer, Henry resolved that his brother Albert would be trained to treat inoperable tumors (once medical knowledge progressed that far). Always, according to family record, the same strict disciplinarian he was from the beginning, Henry now focused on Albert, fourteen years his junior.

Albert followed in his older brother's footsteps in many ways. Like Henry, Albert worked at the Cooper Institute. (Many years later, he recalled a night "when a drunk—'smelling like stale food and stale whiskey'—amazed him by reading Greek as if it had been English.") Albert, too, graduated from City College, and received his medical training at Columbia's College of Physicians and Surgeons. He graduated in 1894, and received many prizes in his final year. Albert followed

Henry to Mount Sinai Hospital, where he served for forty years as one of New York's most distinguished and successful surgeons. Dr Albert A. Berg, known to his colleagues as "A.A.," was a pioneer in the field of abdominal surgery, in which he developed the radical operation for stomach and duodenal ulcers.

During those early years of undoubted hardship there developed an unparalleled affection between the two brothers. They never married, and they shared living quarters to the end of Dr Henry Berg's life. At the height of their career their address was a town house at 10 East 73rd Street.

Apart from their profession they also shared a passion for books. Not medical books but English and American literature as exemplified in the classics and in first editions. The brothers would read to one another from their favorite authors, mostly Dickens and Scott, and they both enjoyed acquiring books (Appendix A describes the highlights of their original collection). But it was Albert who was the more public person and was more interested in building a *collection*, and it is on his story that we will concentrate in the ensuing pages.

The Doctors Berg also shared another passion far more profitable than buying books: they bought real estate. They did so during a period when buying brownstones in the lower East Side of Manhattan was not so difficult as it would seem to us today. Rates were low and income tax in its infancy. Henry Berg was the investor and represented himself in the role of landlord in the United Real Estate Owners' Association and the Greater New York Taxpayers' Association. It was not the

Mount Sinai surgeon who amassed the fortune of $8,104,397 reflected in Albert A. Berg's will probated in 1953, but rather the real estate speculator. The 35-page will bequeathed $5,139,360 to charity.

The largest single bequest, $1,952,672 to New York University, went to establish the Henry W. and Albert A. Berg Institute for Experimental Physiology, Surgery and Pathology at Bellevue Medical Center. Mount Sinai Hospital received $500,000 for the establishment of a research laboratory in memory of Henry. The New York Roman Catholic Archdiocese received $150,000 to be used for the library of the Archbishop Stepinac High School in White Plains; the Protestant Episcopal Diocese of New York received a similar amount. The International College of Surgeons and the New York Academy of Medicine each received $250,000. A similar amount went to New York University, for the establishment of a chair in English and American literature. The University of Pennsylvania received $150,000 to establish a chair for teaching religious thought, including Hebrew.

Finally, $1,750,000 was left to The New York Public Library, rounding out a gift of $250,000 made in Dr Albert A. Berg's lifetime to two million dollars.

Adding the gifts Dr Albert A. Berg made during his lifetime (he survived his brother by twelve years), the fortune the two brothers made would even today be considered large. All Berg donations carry a similar message: the names of the two brothers are always coupled. The parents, Moritz and Josephine Berg, are commemorated in the House of Living Judaism, at 65th Street and Fifth Avenue, a gift made during Albert Berg's lifetime—a final, generous donation to New York.

Truly a rags-to-riches story spun by two men who incorporated great American virtues: individual initiative, self-reliance, and self-help. A belief in democratic values also helped: free education made good by outstanding performance; a universal curiosity encompassing all disciplines; opportunities perceived and exploited. There always remains a tendency for subsequent generations to say: "It was much easier in those days." The record of the Berg brothers would prove the opposite. Not only was it not easy, the obstacles were almost insurmountable. If any generation was up against adversity, it was their generation. Even the briefest outline of two distinct but parallel lives can teach us that lesson.

When Dr Albert A. Berg died on July 1 1950, private and public messages of sympathy from throughout the nation poured out a uniform sentiment of loss. Of the many tributes to Dr Berg, a telegram from the Chairman of the Board of Governors, Hebrew Union College, Jewish Institute of Religion in Cincinnati summed up the universal sense of grief:

> At the death of this great American Jew who as a physician, humanitarian and friend of letters and learning and as a warm hearted human being built for himself during his lifetime a monument of service and of widespread love.

In a poignant phrase, the historian Rebekah Kohut wrote: "He erected his own monuments."

Albert A. Berg

to each and all of his cases is vividly presented in five tributes contributed to a volume consisting largely of scientific medical papers. The one most easily comprehensible to the layman was written by Dr Ernest E. Arnheim in the form of a memoir. In describing Dr Berg's career in detail he wrote:

> Many stories have been told of Dr. Berg's surgical skill. The first characteristic of his surgery which comes to mind was orderliness of procedure. Each operation was made up of a series of steps which followed one another in an orderly sequence, only varying under unusual circumstances. This orderliness of procedure made his surgery a treat for the observer, and simplified the work of the assistant. Operations proceeded step by step, each stage being carried out in a deliberate manner before the next stage was begun. The repetition of steps because they had not been completed in the first instance was eliminated, thus reducing the time of operation, although the individual movements were not rapid. Dr. Berg excelled in the performance of secondary operation in the abdomen in which innumerable adhesions would baffle the average surgeon. . . . He was a man of limitless energy, and he demanded the same of others. His patients were grateful for his tireless, faithful care. His work was done modestly without conceit or self praise.

Dr Arnheim went on to say:

> Dr. Berg was reluctant to try new procedures if those he practiced were of proven efficacy. However, he did not hesitate to change to other methods when the old procedures were proven to be ineffectual. He deserves great credit for adopting the procedure of partial gas-

trectomy for gastric and duodenal ulcer in 1920. He was severely criticized by many American surgeons as being too radical in the surgery of this condition. For years these surgeons continued to practice the operation of gastroenterostomy, and now we find that the operation of partial gastrectomy is the accepted surgical procedure for gastric and duodenal ulcer, and the operative technique which he proposed in 1923 is now widely practiced.

From 1914 to 1934, Dr Berg's prominence as a surgeon in New York was evident to the medical profession and to thousands of his patients and their families.

On May 19 1934, when Dr Berg's colleagues at Mount Sinai Hospital honored his forty years of service, Dr Bernard Eliasberg said (with some facetiousness) in his dinner speech:

> We are assembled tonight to render honor to Dr. Albert A. Berg. This season marks the fortieth year of his association with Mount Sinai Hospital. The Jews do things by forties—forty years in the wilderness—forty years at Mount Sinai. Forty years of noble work in a noble profession—forty years of unceasing and untiring service to his fellow men. Forty years is a considerable segment of our span of life. How many of us have been able to give as much? Very few indeed, and I ask further: how many of us have been able to get so much? None.

Long after his death, former patients, often generations apart, come to visit the Berg Collection in The New York Public Library, to stand under his portrait in silent or not-so-silent tribute. They pour out stories of fast action and steady healing.

Long after their own operations, old patients came to retell how Dr Berg had saved their lives. Their number decreased over the years, but now younger people come to recall what grandpa or great-uncle told them about a legendary doctor, whose only enemies were reported to have been death and cancer.

In commenting on a dangerous surgical technique, Dr Leon Ginzburg remarked:

> At present operations of this scope and magnitude are daily carried to a successful conclusion by surgeons still in the formal training period of their careers. This in itself is a tribute to the thoroughness with which the pioneer surgeons in this field, of whom Dr. Berg was emphatically one, accomplished their task. There is nothing so indicative of progress in surgery as when the "tours de force" of yesterday have become the commonplaces of today.

# III

The Collector

*Book-collecting. It's a great game.
Anybody with ordinary intelligence
can play it*—A. E. Newton *This
Book Collecting Game* (1928)

These books, manuscripts, and letters, together with the appointments in this room, were the dear friends of my late brother and myself. In presenting them to you and the Trustees of the Public Library of our City, and through you to the public it is with the pleasant anticipation that their new friends will use them and love them as much as we did.

These were the words spoken by Albert A. Berg on October 11 1940, during the formal presentation of the Henry W. and Albert A. Berg Collection in Memory of Henry W. Berg. Governor Herbert H. Lehman and Mayor Fiorello H. LaGuardia were among those present at the ceremony, which demonstrated Dr Berg's life-long conviction that a citizen of New York owes a debt to the public good.

Nothing that Dr Berg did was unplanned or haphazard, and during the summer preceding the ceremony, a room in the Central Building of The New York Public Library was furnished according to plans drawn up by one of New York's finest architectural firms, Eggers and Higgins, at a cost of $50,000. Austrian oak was imported to panel a reading room surrounded by fluted Corinthian columns. Objets d'art from Dr Berg's home on East 73rd Street were to be accommodated in a specially designed cabinet. A terra-cotta figure of Moses holding the Tablet of the Law by the Renaissance artist Giovanni della Robbia (1469–1527?) graced the lunette above the front door.

A portrait of Henry W. Berg by Ellen Emmett Rand, commissioned after his death, was hung in the center of the east wall with the inscription: "Doctor Henry W. Berg 1858–1938 Physician and Educator; worker for professional and civic welfare; collector, lover of books."

The fitted bookcases housed the original Berg Collection, amounting to some three thousand books and manuscripts.

Dr Berg's gift to the Library was accompanied by a donation of $250,000 made on February 6 1940; the donor stipulated that it was to be "kept in perpetuity and the income thereof shall be used for the salary of the librarian of this collection, the proper maintenance, care and binding of the books and other objects of the collection, and the purchase, when possible, of additional books similar in character to those now in the collection."

During this inaugural year Dr Berg saw and grasped a unique opportunity. A great private collection formed by W. T. H. Howe, President of the American Book Company, came into the market after the collector's death in 1939, and Dr Berg purchased it in its entirety for the Berg Collection. Mr Howe had built his collection for over forty years at the reputed cost of over two million dollars. Thus, the three hundred distinguished guests at the presentation ceremony of the Berg Collection also celebrated this new acquisition of 16,000 books and manuscripts, the majority of which were outstanding research and museum pieces in English and American literature.

Mr Howe's collection also included Charles Dickens's desk, which was placed directly under Henry Berg's portrait. To accompany the desk, the chair Dickens used in the office of his periodical publication *Household Words* was also on view. (Mayor LaGuardia sat in it that afternoon and promptly broke the caning.)

What the President of the Board of Trustees of The New York Public Library described as Dr Berg's other "princely gift" had been considered to be one of two outstanding collections of English and American literature remaining in private hands.

W. T. H. Howe (1874–1939) shared a common trait with some other great collectors: he was secretive and shunned publicity. Little, therefore, was known of his collection and collecting habits outside a small circle of the book trade and personal friends. Among his contemporaries he was in a unique position to collect manuscripts of living writers. First as a salesman and, during the final decade of his life, as President of the American Book Company based in Cincinnati, Howe knew personally such writers as the Irish poets W. B. Yeats, James Stephens, and A. E. (William George Russell). His estate at Mentor, Kentucky, was named "Freelands" after the novel of his friend John Galsworthy. At Freelands the use of Howe's library was liberally offered to all who visited him.

The highlights of the Howe collection read like a roll call of great works: one of—then—eleven known copies of Edgar Allan Poe's *Tamerlane* with the dedication copy of *The Raven* to Elizabeth Barrett Browning and her letter of acceptance with it; the first edition of Thomas Gray's *An Elegy Wrote in a Country Church Yard;* the Rosebery copy of Keats's *Endymion* presented by the author to Leigh Hunt; a water color by Charlotte Brontë; eleven Dickens works used during his reading tours and annotated by him to serve as his own prompt copies; the manuscript of George Gissing's *Demos;* the manuscript of Charles Lamb's *The Old Benchers of the Inner Temple*, an essay of "Elia."

Howe was born and grew up in Boston. He spent considerable time in Concord, Massachusetts, and his collection is particularly strong in the New England authors. He had letters from Emerson to Carlyle; Thoreau was well represented. He owned the entire correspondence between Whitman and W. D. O'Connor, and the early American authors James K. Paulding, Charles Brockden Brown, and James P. Kennedy were there in first editions. However, like the Berg brothers, Howe concentrated on Dickens and Thackeray. In some great sales he acted with dispatch and success. His collection of Thackeray was particularly strong in letters, drawings, and manuscripts. In a 1941 publication, before the Howe Collection could be catalogued, the great combined gift to The New York Public Library was described as possessing "the double attraction of utility and charm."

These dual attributes, while true and sound, would not have satisfied Dr Berg: he knew that he had placed his growing collection on a solid base. With the arrival of the Howe collection, he asked for a second room. Part of what was then the Lenox Gallery was assigned by the Board for that purpose and the donor had the walls panelled and the room fitted up with book and exhibition cases, permitting "the display of the paintings on the side walls with no essential change from the former arrangement."

In a vast room Dr Berg foresaw periodically changing exhibitions to show off his treasures to a vast public. The first one, appropriately devoted to Charles Dickens, opened on December 16 1941. By that time a third founding collection, that of Owen D. Young, had been presented to the Library by Dr Berg and Mr Young. Dr Berg then asked for, and received, a third room.

But back on Inauguration Day, October 11 1940, Dr Berg had no other plans than to house his own and the Howe collection in two separate rooms—separate but equal under the name "Berg Collection." The most memorable address of the day was delivered by a personal friend, Governor of New York Herbert H. Lehman. In thanking Dr Berg for his generosity to the City, the Governor went on to describe his personal friendship of some thirty years and the close bond which linked the two Berg brothers. In the Governor's opinion, their library was,

> one more link in the great chain of civic devotion, patriotism and service which Dr. Berg has fashioned throughout his exceptionally valuable life and which

will bind the people of our city and state to him in loving appreciation so long as memory lasts.

In his remarks, he also emphasized what has since become increasingly evident, that,

> this collection which represents years of effort is one of the most outstanding in all the world. It contains most of the important works of the great authors in poetry and prose during the last four centuries of English and American literature. The value to the student and the research worker of a collection in English and American literature of this importance cannot be exaggerated. New York and the entire nation are indeed fortunate to acquire this historic library.

The strength of the Howe collection had brought to The New York Public Library what its President, the Hon. Frank L. Polk, described to the press on September 20 1940, a manuscript and book collection that "surpassed any acquisition [by the Library] since the consolidation of the Astor and Lenox Libraries and the Tilden Trust in 1895." The generosity of Dr Berg, and the acquisitive genius of the Library's epoch-making director, Harry Miller Lydenberg, did not stop with the purchase of the Howe collection. On May 5 1941, a front-page headline of *The New York Times* read: "Young Collection of Rare Volumes Is Gift to Library. 10,000 Literary Treasures Are Joint Donation of Founder and Dr Albert A. Berg." With it, said the Library's spokesman, the institution became "one of the primary sources for literary research in the world."

Owen D. Young (1874–1962) found a perfect partner in Dr Berg when he went public with his private collection. In a career that took him from a farm in Van Hornesville, New York, to Chairmanship of the Board of the General Electric Company, from Boston University Law School to the international conference tables that drew up the Dawes Plan of 1924, he also devoted his life to public service under five Presidents and, in New York State, to membership on the Board of Regents from 1934 to 1946. The gift of the Young collection, containing over 15,000 items, was presented jointly (the arrangements between the two collectors were not disclosed).

Mr Young shared the bibliophilic acumen which distinguished a whole generation of collectors, and the advantages afforded to them in having a vast market in which to buy rare books and manuscripts. The first thirty years of this century witnessed the dispersal of extraordinary private collections which ultimately wound up in public institutions. At the height of the Depression, when the market in rare books surprisingly commanded the highest prices, the opportunities to acquire some real treasures multiplied for those who did have the money to do so. Mr Young had acquired, primarily during the 20s, a peerless collection of many unique or extremely rare items. He was in that best company of private collectors whose names, Hoe, Huth, Kern, Clawson, Chew, Hagen, Newton, are part of collecting history.

When on May 8 1941, Dr Berg, Owen D. Young, and The New York Public Library concluded all the formalities of transfer, the Berg Collection gained global significance. It acquired its second copy of Poe's *Tamerlane;* one of the largest archival collections of Fanny Burney, the eighteenth-century English novelist, containing her manuscript diaries and some

2,500 letters, together with the manuscript of *Evelina;* many Dickens items, among them an invaluable source, his memoranda book; the last letter of John Keats to his beloved Fanny Brawne; numerous manuscripts of Burns, Walter Scott, Coleridge, Mark Twain, and Lewis Carroll. There were a peerless collection of Rudyard Kipling and rare examples of eighteenth-century classics, including Alexander Pope's copy of the *Poems* of Milton, whose *Comus* and *Paradise Lost* in first editions, great rarities of English literature, were also present. Among the museum pieces, William Blake's *Songs of Innocence* and *Europe a Prophecy* took their rightful place.

When the joint gift of Owen D. Young's golden collection was announced, Dr Berg revealed that they had never met "prior to the day that they got together to complete the transaction by signing the agreement." He added, "we had heard of each other as collectors, of course." The spirit that governed the two individuals seems to be very similar, because **Dr Berg** continued to say that "Mr. Young has said to others that he felt he was accumulating his store of literary treasures, not for his own benefit, but as a curator, and that he eventually hoped to turn them over to one or more institutions of learning."

Dr Berg and Owen D. Young made a pair of happy givers while a library official described institutional pleasure in saying: "You take a look at what is in the boxes, and just sit back and gasp!"

The Berg, Howe, and Young collections were not the only gifts that made headlines during Dr Berg's lifetime. In 1943 and 1944, jointly with the book dealer Gabriel Wells, Dr

Berg presented to his Collection the manuscripts of Byron's "The Curse of Minerva," J. M. Barrie's *The Little Minister*, Sir Walter Scott's last, unfinished work, *The Siege of Malta*, and Bernard Shaw's first play, *Widowers' Houses*, together with two early printings by William Caxton. Coleridge's 1814–25 "clasped vellum" manuscript notebook became public property first in manuscript and decades later in printed form. When in his will Dr Berg provided the remainder of the endowment fund (totalling two million dollars) which was necessary for the upkeep and further growth of his library, he exercised extraordinary foresight, and one that all donors to public institutions might wish to emulate.

During his lifetime, and in his will, Dr Berg left instructions and made provisions about the care of the Collection, the most touching of which was that a portrait of himself be hung next to that of his brother. Jean Spencer painted the institutional portrait from a photograph of Dr Berg, in which he holds a Young treasure, Blake's *Europe a Prophecy*, and in which, because it postdated the death of Henry, he no longer wears the habitual red carnation in his buttonhole. The portrait was unveiled on November 8 1951 at a public presentation by the Executors of Dr Berg's estate. Among the four speakers of the day there appeared a young scholar, John D. Gordan, who, as curator of the Berg Collection, spoke of Dr Berg as a collector. He also opened his sixteenth exhibition, entitled *First Fruits: First Books by American Authors 1807–1915*.

John D. Gordan (1907–1968), at that time in his forties, was tall, handsome, and in full charge of the Berg Collection (he had consulted with the founder on all major purchases since coming to the Library in 1940). He announced, soon after Dr Berg's death, that following instructions in Dr Berg's will, air conditioning would gradually be installed in the three rooms of the Collection (work was completed in 1963). He pointed to the large number of visitors in the Exhibition Room where, during a six-month exhibition of Robert and Elizabeth Barrett Browning in 1946, 68,000 people came to read and to learn. An average of 270 to 300 visitors daily was not unusual. The attraction during those days was not just in the novelty of a newly opened great collection: the generous presentation of literary material with perceptive and urbane notes by the curator provided the visitor with an appealing opportunity to study and enjoy at leisure manuscripts and first editions of great works, many of them never before available to public view.

Before joining The New York Public Library, John D. Gordan, a Virginian, had received his Ph.D. from Harvard in 1939, where he had been an instructor for nine years. He was one of the first Conrad scholars in the United States. Dr Gordan was Berg curator from the Collection's earliest days in the public institution. From 1942 he served in the Navy as lieutenant commander, and returned in 1946 to continue his work in advising Dr Berg on purchases. Dr Berg, a suspicious man by nature, trusted his curator absolutely. He was not always an easy public donor, but both men were reasonable, and reason prevailed. For many years following Dr Berg's death, it was Dr Gordan's unfailing memory which could throw light on obscure circumstances surrounding an acquisition or explain why a particular item had found its way into the Collection. It was Dr Gordan's unmatched wit which kept some of the best stories alive and, until his death in 1968, hardly a day passed that the Berg curator did not invoke Dr Berg's name.

Dr Berg, the private collector gone public, enlarged on his purpose both in deeds and in words. When, after the purchase of the Howe collection, he was asked how much he had paid, he refused to say. "A book collector is just cut out on those damn fool lines," he said, adding, "he never tries to remember how much he paid for an expensive book."

In describing the beginnings of the Berg brothers as collectors, however, Dr Berg became more expansive:

> After we started collecting we made a solemn promise not to pay more than $100 for a book. Then the limit was raised to $200, to $300, then $500. I'll never forget the time I paid more than $1,000 for a book. It was for the Salisbury edition of Goldsmith's *Vicar of Wakefield*, first edition, the only one with the last blank leaf in signature. I paid $1,450 for it. My first conquest in rare editions came as a young doctor. I had been brought up on Dickens, my favorite, and I knew every character in his books. So I went into Dutton's then on Fifth Avenue in the Fifties, and paid $100 for Dickens's *Little Dorrit*. I thought I built a good collection of Dickens during the years until I saw Howe's—he was the man who paid $19,000 for a letter from Elizabeth Barrett Browning to Poe. Howe had a wonderful collection, Dickens and others. That's one reason I bought it. If the Howe Collection had been broken, it could never be put together again.

Dr Albert A. Berg holding one of the Young treasures, Blake's *Europe:* oil portrait by Jean Spencer (1951) from a 1941 photograph

Dr Henry W. Berg: oil portrait by Ellen Emmett Rand (1940), from a photograph (ca. 1930s)

Josephine Schiff Berg holding her daughter Fanny, with her other children ca. 1870 (*left to right*) Abraham, Adelia, Amelia (Millie), and Henry Woolfe (photograph: *gift of Gertrude Willett, 1961*)

Henry W. and Albert A. Berg (*seated, second and third from left*), most likely in a family portrait (ca. 1900)

Albert A. Berg as a young doctor (*seated, second from left*)

Albert A. Berg on one of his 1920s excursions into the Great Smokies (photograph: *gift of Mrs Flora Stieglitz Straus, 1969*)

One of Dr Albert A. Berg's many philanthropies: a memorial to his parents, the Moritz and Josephine Berg Memorial House of Living Judaism, the seven-story national center of Reform Judaism at 835 Fifth Avenue (at 65th Street) completed in 1951

> *Poets generally, who wrote before the Restoration (1660). Before I say, that this premature warm and sunny day, anteceding Spring, called forth the following*
>
> Strain in the manner of G. Herbert — which might be entitled, The Alone Most Dear: a Complaint of Jacob to Rachel as in the tenth year of his Service he saw in her and fancied that he saw Symptoms of Alienation. — It was Fancy.
>
> ---
>
> All nature seems at work. Slugs leave their lair;
> The Bees are stirring; Birds are on the wing;
> And WINTER slumbering in the open air
> Wears on his smiling face a dream of Spring.
> And I, the while, the sole unbusy thing,
> Nor honey make, nor pair, nor build, nor sing.
>
> Yet well I ken the banks, where *Amaranths blow,
> Have traced the fount whence streams of Nectar flow.
> Bloom, O ye Amaranths! bloom for whom ye may —
> For me ye bloom not! Glide, rich streams! away!
>
> *literally rendered is Flower Fadeless, or never-fading — from the Greek a not and maraino, to wither.

A 1944 gift of **Dr Berg**'s (jointly with Gabriel Wells): the beautiful "clasped vellum" 1814—25 notebook of Samuel Taylor Coleridge open to page 169 with the first draft of his 1825 sonnet "Work without Hope"

THE
LIFE
AND
STRANGE SURPRIZING
ADVENTURES
OF
ROBINSON CRUSOE,
Of *YORK*, MARINER:

Who lived Eight and Twenty Years,
all alone in an un-inhabited Island on the
Coast of AMERICA, near the Mouth of
the Great River of OROONOQUE;

Having been cast on Shore by Shipwreck, where-
in all the Men perished but himself.

WITH
An Account how he was at last as strangely deli-
ver'd by PYRATES.

Written by Himself.

LONDON:
Printed for W. TAYLOR at the *Ship* in *Pater-Noster-
Row.* MDCCXIX.

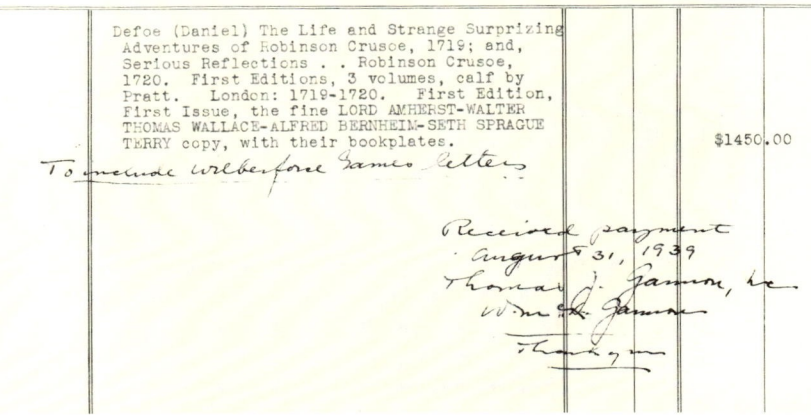

One of the works in the original Berg Collection: from the first volume of the first edition, first issue of Defoe's *Robinson Crusoe: The Life and Strange Surprizing Adventures of Robinson Crusoe* ... (1719); with the 1939 bill to Dr Berg from the book dealer Thomas J. Gannon, Inc.

The Berg Collection Reading Room, with a
view of the south wall plaque commemorating
the Judge and Mrs Samuel D. Levy Memorial
Publication Fund and, over the entrance, of
the *Moses* by Giovanni della Robbia, a
fifteenth-century glazed terra cotta
formerly in the Berg home

IV

The Trustee

Speech is the messenger of the heart.
                            The Talmud

In Dr Berg's institutional obituary notice written by John D. Gordan we read:

> A man of Dr. Berg's comprehensive intelligence and inexhaustible energy was ready to give more than financial support to an institution in which he took an interest. He gave himself. In October, 1941, he became a member of the Board of Trustees of the Library. His particular interest was in the Library Committee and his usefulness and importance to the Committee is revealed in his having served as Chairman from 1944 to the time of his death. Never before had the chairmanship been held by one man for longer than one year without rotation. At the time of his death he had also served as a member of the Executive Committee for five months.
>
> It was in the difficult work of the Library's centennial drive for funds in 1949 that he showed his most unselfish devotion. As Chairman of the Friends of the Library, he made spirited appeals to large civic groups, especially to women's organizations. As a member of Governor Dewey's Committee on Library Aid he worked tirelessly for financial assistance to the libraries of New York State.

Dr Berg's contributions to The New York Public Library were in the long tradition of support from New York's most distinguished citizens. The Astor Library, older of the founding libraries of what became The New York Public Library, had itself been the legacy of John Jacob Astor, who died on March 29 1848. His, the first free public library in New York, opened on Lafayette Place on January 9 1854, with almost 80,000 books in its collections. In 1895 The New York Public Library was formed by the consolidation of the Astor Library, the Lenox Library (founded by James Lenox in 1870), and the Samuel J. Tilden Trust. The greatly expanded collections were added to over the years with the aid of endowment funds from John D. Rockefeller, Jr, Payne Whitney, Anna M. Harkness, Edward S. Harkness, and many others. In 1911 the New York Public Library's nine-million-dollar Central Building, consolidating what Harry Miller Lydenberg, the Library's Director and historian, termed, "many isolated, independent efforts toward a common end, the public weal," opened to the admiration of the citizens of New York.

By April 25 1949, *The New York Times* was able to report on the Library's centennial party:

> Any strange glint that a visitor to the staid precincts of the Forty-second Street Library may find today in the eyes of Socrates, Washington Irving or the other plaster busts there should be attributed to the sort of party that might happen once in a hundred years—and in this case it did.

However, it was not only music that echoed in the marble halls the night of the centennial celebration. Morris Hadley,

President of the Board of Trustees from 1943 to 1958, launched the first fund drive in the Library's history. The goal was ten million dollars. During its first century the Library relied on donations from private individuals for maintaining The Research Libraries (they were then known as the Reference Department) and on the taxpayers' money to support the lending services (there were sixty-five branches operating in 1948).

Time was running out on the wealthy individuals who in the past were able to support most of the non-profit institutions in New York. Mr Hadley made his points by saying:

> Catastrophe cannot be avoided by calling on a few individuals to contribute the important sums we need. Unless thousands of people, business firms and organizations contribute to the support of the Central Reference Library, its resources will sink into mediocrity.
>
> New York has a great library today because at critical times there have always been citizens who acted with greatness. Every step of its development was conceived and made possible by individual men and women of more than ordinary character and ability, who loved books and their community, and found in the library a means of making knowledge available to all.

As Chairman of the Friends during this crucial campaign, Dr Berg helped establish that tradition of broad support that would be essential to the survival of the Library in the future.

Dr Berg had been elected in 1943 to be a National Regent in Surgery, International College of Surgeons. It was not a mere shift in title when he became a charter member of the Library Trustees Foundation of New York State, which received a charter from the New York State Board of Regents on February 26 1949. It was a shift in Dr Berg's activities and the final public-spirited act on behalf of The New York Public Library.

Having gained national prominence as a physician, Dr Berg took up a role in the Empire State's educational system of paramount importance. The President of the newly organized Library Trustees Foundation, Thomas H. McKaig of Buffalo, reported that the six hundred public libraries in the state were "collapsing." In notes jotted down on stationery printed for the Office of the President of the Collège International de Chirurgiens, Dr Berg made some points:

> Local communities cannot afford expensive books that are infrequently used. Outside of NY City 10 counties provide library service to 75% or more of their population 30 counties provide 50–75%; 11 counties less than 50%; 1½ million people in the State have no library service.

Dr Berg described the goal in a vision thirty years have not been able to turn into reality:

> The goals to be achieved in an adequate library service a) all citizens of State of NY should be able to get as many books etc. as they need b) the citizens should have the services of professional trained librarians.

He found the present state of affairs unacceptable and, he believed, he was in a position to change it. President McKaig was less sanguine in declaring that the goal of the campaign was to put libraries "in a condition of minimum financial security necessary to support democracy."

On September 21 1949, Dr Berg wrote to a friend:

> The regional library matter has grown very much. The N. Y. State Board of Regents incorporated an activity known as the N.Y. State Library Trustees Foundation of which I am the Vice President, and the Governor has appointed a N.Y. State Library Comm. to which he has appointed me as a member—and we are very actively engaged in work. . . .

On May 25 1950, he added:

> It was very thoughtful of you to write me concerning the passage of the bill for State Aid to Libraries. The bill will give to the N.Y. City Reference and N.Y. City Bronx and Staten Island Circulating Libraries a yearly sum of 700 thousand dollars. This amount will help materially to get us a balanced budget. It has been a hard fight but the Governor and Legislature at length saw eye to eye with us. This victory for the Libraries of the Entire State came after almost three years of continuous effort but it is a satisfaction to know that I accomplished in this period of time what the N.Y. State Library Association and other Library interests had not been able to do in fifty years. This is the beginning. I am sure that in one or two decades from now the State budget for Libraries will equal that of Education!— Regional Libraries will follow as soon as we establish a Statewide County Library System. The beginning has been made—The future (?)

To us, thirty years later, that final (?) is still there. However, Dr Berg, the lobbyist in Albany, died two months later in the knowledge that his vested interest in The New York Public Library brought dividends to the entire state.

Dr Berg belonged to that generation of New Yorkers who believed in free education for all. He believed in the individual value of each and every educated citizen. He was going to make sure that they multiply in numbers and in wisdom. Had he lived one more decade, he could have witnessed personally the expansion and growth of libraries.

He would have enjoyed it very much.

V

The Man

*Secret and self-contained and solitary
as an oyster*—Charles Dickens
A Christmas Carol (1843)

Dr Berg was six feet tall, slender, and forbidding. His voice was high pitched. "Intense, bearded bibliophile of sixty-eight" was Geoffrey Hellman's description of him in *The New Yorker* in 1941. He was "smoking a small Cuban cigar in a crooked holder specially cut for him." Colleagues, and Mount Sinai Hospital nurses, often confirmed Dr Berg's regular habits, as described in *The New Yorker*: "He rises at six, breakfasts at seven, goes up to the Mt. Sinai Hospital, where he is a consulting surgeon, at eight, and operates all morning. From twelve-thirty to two-thirty, except for a few minutes for lunch, he holds office hours," and after more work most of the afternoon and evening "reads either medical or general literature until one or two in the morning. He has three canaries, all called Dickie, and at nights turns on the radio for the benefit of the one in his bedroom. 'I let him hear music. It keeps him in form,' he said. 'No boogie-woogie.'"

Dr Berg led a strict and spartan life. He could have afforded a car, and even a driver, but he preferred taking the bus. Colleagues at the hospital, a mile and a half from the doctor's home, called the Fifth Avenue bus Dr Berg's green car. Some joked about how he could have saved himself a nickel by taking the Madison Avenue bus. He frequently entertained colleagues during formal dinners in his home on East 73rd Street, during which the topic was surgery or the discussion of a rare item the collector had recently bought. There was, or so it has been reported, little conversation at these dinners because Dr Berg was the speaker.

After the Berg Collection was transferred from East 73rd Street to 42nd Street and Fifth Avenue, Dr Berg's weekly routine included two or three visits a week with the curator in order to discuss pending purchases. John D. Gordan, the first curator of the Berg Collection, noted: "As it so frequently does, the act of turning a private collection into a public benefaction whetted Doctor Albert's ardor." Dr Gordan went on to describe his early relationship with Dr Berg: "It was my happy responsibility to read dealers' and auction catalogues, to note items of interest to the Collection, and to report to the Doctor. He was as keenly interested in the details of purchase of a $100 item as of one costing thousands." The more expensive books were for the public Berg Collection: "I use dollar books now," remarked Dr Berg at the presentation of the Owen D. Young collection in May 1941.

During the summers starting in the early 1920s, and until his brother's death in 1938, Dr Berg spent regular vacations in his camp in the Great Smokies, where he used to ride forty to fifty miles a day and shoot bear and wildcat. The only surviving photograph provided by one of his partners during these occasions is accompanied by the comment: "This picture certainly doesn't resemble the dapper gentleman with the red carnation that we knew."

But then, after the death of his brother on December 22 1938, nothing resembled the past. Dr Berg stopped wearing the fresh red carnation in his buttonhole daily, for which he was known all over New York and which he wore even in surgery. In their home, over Dr Berg's desk, a photograph of Henry's consulting room, left as it was when he died, served as a reminder of Dr Henry Woolfe Berg's work as a physician. On the mantelpiece rested the last of the stiff collars and cravats Henry had worn until he died.

While still young, at the age of sixty-two, Dr Albert Berg retired as attending surgeon at Mount Sinai, although he continued to perform surgery. The then City Commissioner of Hospitals was quoted in *The New York Times* as saying: "If I had twenty Bergs I could raise the standards of our hospitals materially. If I had forty Bergs I could transform them that nevermore would there be any doubt where the center of the medical world is."

For Dr Berg after the death of his brother, a new leaf had turned. It was then that he decided to go public. In February 1940 he established the Berg Collection; in September 1940 he added the W. T. H. Howe collection; in May 1941 he added the Owen D. Young collection. In October 1941 Dr Berg became a member of the Board of Trustees of The New York Public Library and in 1944 he headed its Library Committee.

Dr Gordan explained Dr Berg's devotion to the Berg Collection: "Once the memorial to Dr. Henry W. had been established and their private collection turned over to the public,

Dr. A. A. found his desire to build up the collection strengthened. Quite possibly, since he would now be buying material for an institution instead of for his own library, his dislike of self-indulgence was no longer a deterrent to large expenditure. His native shrewdness, furthermore, prompted him to take advantage of opportunities to purchase two great collections *en bloc*."

Another facet of Dr Berg's devotion to his books was described by his old friend and patient Carl H. Pforzheimer. Mr Pforzheimer recalled his "slight operation with a local anesthetic, when out of the vague distance came Dr. Berg's voice." It seems Dr Berg was asking Mr Pforzheimer if a certain book of his had "such-and-such a point." As Mr Pforzheimer explained, "the devotion to rare books was always with him, and his skill in surgery was so sure that even while operating he could discuss some bookish point that was lurking in his mind."

In 1941 City College in its citation that accompanied the Townsend Harris Medal recognized its 1891 alumnus as follows:

> The hands of men and the minds that direct them have been more often turned to deeds of cruelty than to acts of enduring kindness. Those men, therefore, who, being possessed of great skills, have enriched the minds and healed the bodies of their fellows have been, as Baudelaire called them, beacons in the murky night of man's inhumanity to man. You are one of *les phares*. In the great hospital which you served long and brilliantly, the skill of your magic hands brought many back from the shadow of death. In the Public Library

> you have set an inexhaustible feast before the hungry in spirit. You are the Sir Thomas Bodley of New York: a very Maecenas who has gladdened the days of living men and endowed the ages. In you Alma Mater finds particular reason to rejoice.

From 1945 to 1948 Dr Berg served as President of the International College of Surgeons, of which he was a founder. During the sixth international meeting in Rome, Dr Berg was received by Pope Pius XII in a private audience. Of his visit he wrote:

> My audience of forty minutes alone with the Pope was extremely stimulating and spiritual. It well repaid in itself the trip to Rome. Sitting with him in his study and conversing with him for so long a time permitted me to realize what a wonderful man he is. He is by far the most spiritual brilliant, sweet, noble man I have ever met and I left his presence with reverence and great admiration.

The University of Rome demonstrated its admiration for Dr Berg in bestowing on him during that visit an honorary degree in surgery.

Dr Berg's last public appearance was on Sunday, June 25 1950, when he attended the groundbreaking ceremony of the new national home of Reform Judaism on the southeast corner of Fifth Avenue and 65th Street. He provided a generous, undisclosed sum, described as "the largest single contribution to any Jewish religious body in our generation." The building, which upon its completion won an architectural award, is known as the Moritz and Josephine Berg Memorial. Dr Berg was by then a very sick man and did not get out of the car from which he observed the ceremony.

It seems to us now that 10 East 73rd Street, the private home of two brothers, became too confining after the death of the elder. While Albert guarded the memory of Henry, he made every effort to secure his own survival in the philanthropic gifts he left behind. By the time of Dr Albert Berg's death, twelve years after his brother's, he could leave with the certainty that his own name and that of his family would outlast his lifetime. He personally supervised the casting of names in bronze and engraved in wood and in stone. The bronze plaque decorating the Fifth Avenue wall of the Periodicals Room in The New York Academy of Medicine, naming it the Henry W. and Albert A. Berg wing, and the gilt lettering in wood on the panelling of the Henry W. and Albert A. Berg Collection of English and American Literature, bear witness not only to the workmanship of the carver's art, but also to the careful wording of each phrase. In the Berg Collection a second plaque commemorates the donation of Dr Berg's sister Mrs Millie Levy, who, together with her husband Judge Samuel D. Levy, left an endowment fund for publications based on materials in her brothers' public collection.

From comments made by Dr Berg's contemporaries and published in the press, we know of his reasonableness and of the praise given for his "instinctive individualism." We are told of his "foresight which defies analysis." In another tribute, written by Dr Duncan Macpherson in February 1950, we who have become familiar with Dr Berg only in our role of public caretakers can recognize the following qualities as a key to his manifold success: "self reliance nurtured by successive achievements, by talents with their roots deeply planted and flowering through many traits and tendencies— an example to the laggard and to the vanguard, he has earned the esteem of his colleagues in our profession, of the lay elect and the gratitude of the less fortunate by outstanding service. A man of self confidence without conceit. A man with many friends—and I hope some enemies—who met obstacles and surmounted them leaving footprints on the sands of time. Still achieving, still pursuing. A helpful friend. A good citizen. A good man."

To this generation, by now twice removed, it is clear that having received much Dr Berg was happy to give all. Having returned to New York City the sum of his possessions, he truly did all he did with his might.

References

Copies of works quoted or reproduced are in the Berg Collection unless otherwise noted (Box numbers followed by roman numerals refer to the location of material in the Albert A. Berg papers). For an overview of the Collection, see the *Dictionary Catalog of the Henry W. and Albert A. Berg Collection of English and American Literature* 5 vols (Boston: G. K. Hall & Co 1969), *First Supplement* 1 vol (1975), *Second Supplement* 1 vol (1983)—in the entries, the letters "H," "Y," and "B" identify works from the Howe, Young, and original Berg collections—and *Guide to the Research Collections of The New York Public Library* comp Sam P. Williams et al. (Chicago: American Library Association 1975) 79-80. The Young collection in particular is described in Lola L. Szladits *Owen D. Young: Book Collector* intro Josephine Young Case (New York: The New York Public Library and Readex Books 1974). If there is more than one reference to a work, the full publishing information is given in the first reference, and an abbreviated form of the title is used thereafter.

I

Page

10 "Help Wanted": Family stories on the Bergs' early life are taken from the 1939 typescript (8 p) by their grand-niece Jean Pinanski "Dr. Henry W. Berg—Physician and Citizen" (Box III, gift of Gertrude Willett, 1950).

11 When a drunk: Albert A. Berg, in New York *Herald Tribune* (September 23 1940) 13.

14 At the death: Lester A. Jaffe, telegram, July 5 1950, in the memorial album collected and bound by Mrs Samuel D. Levy (presented February 15 1951).

He erected: A tribute by Rebekah Kohut in the memorial album.

References, continued

V

39 Intense, bearded: [Geoffrey Hellman] "Donor" *The New Yorker* 17 (May 24 1941) 12.
40 As it so frequently: John D. Gordan "Dr. Berg as a Collector" *Bulletin* 55 (December 1951) 578–79.
  I use dollar books now: Albert A. Berg in *The New York Times* (May 5 1941) 19.
41 If I had: Dr Sigismund S. Goldwater, in *The New York Times* (July 2 1950) 24.
  Once the memorial: Gordan "A Doctor's Benefaction" 306.
42 slight operation: Carl H. Pforzheimer "Dr. Berg as a Friend" *Bulletin* 55 (December 1951) 579.
  The hands of men: quoted in Bernard Kreissman "The Berg Collection" *The City College Alumnus* 45 i (October 1949) 16.
43 My audience: Albert A. Berg, letter to Mrs Leonard B Scofield, June 17 1948 (Box I).
  the largest single contribution: Dr Maurice N. Eisendrath, in *The New York Times* (December 14 1949) 35.
44 plaque: The Berg and Levy plaques in the Berg Collection are shown in photographs reproduced following page 32 above.
  instinctive individualism: Dr John Mulholland, in *New York University Medical Quarterly* 8 iv (Winter 1952) 7.
45 self reliance: Duncan Macpherson *What Not* (Privately Printed, February 1950).

Appendix A

53 check list: [Check List of Works in the Original Berg Collection], untitled, occasionally annotated, and uncorrected typescript (87 p) that accompanied the original gift in 1940, most likely prepared under Dr Berg's direction after August 30 1939 (the date of the *Robinson Crusoe* acquisition listed)—

References, continued

"NYPL, RD [Reference Department], Special Collections, Berg": Box no. 7, The New York Public Library Archives, Rare Books and Manuscripts Division.
54 William H. Robinson: "Gift of the . . . Berg Collection" 880.
discovery: "Gift of the . . . Berg Collection" 880–81.
55 discrimination: William Gladstone's remarks were used by Dr Berg in preliminary notes for a talk (Box II), probably the 1949 one referred to below.
56 for study: Albert A. Berg, in manuscript notes for a talk on book collecting delivered to the Scarsdale, New York Women's Club on April 20 1949 (Box II).

Appendix A

Some Highlights of the Original Berg Collection

An early love of Dickens and Thackeray introduced the Berg brothers to the particular pleasures of reading and by the first decade of this century to the enthusiasm for book collecting (see Chapter IV above). Reading aloud and talking about books were always an important part of their life at home in the comfortable town house on East 73rd Street off Fifth Avenue—and books and art works filled their third-floor Library and Music Room and the doctors' own offices on the lower floors. From the occasional records of the brothers' early collecting that have survived in the Berg papers and in the check list that accompanied the gift of the original collection of some 3,500 volumes in 1940, one can reconstruct the story of a remarkably diversified gentleman's library with a concentration in nineteenth-century English literature (Dickens accounted for almost a tenth of the holdings, with Scott and Thackeray heavily represented). They had the collected works of the best authors (Heine in English, for one) and choice examples of the earliest issues of great works from the whole range of English literature, especially from the seventeenth to the nineteenth century. From earlier periods, Spenser was represented with good copies of first editions of *The Faerie Queene* (1590-96) and, more surprisingly, *Colin Clouts Come Home Againe* (1595); and there were a few modern authors such as Conrad or Eugene O'Neill (a signed copy of a 1928 edition of *The Emperor Jones*) and inscribed copies of novels by the Bergs'

HENRY W. BERG, now in THE NEW YORK PUBLIC LIBRARY, and to cause said painting to be hung in a suitable place in the space set aside in THE NEW YORK PUBLIC LIBRARY which houses the collection provided for by the "HENRY W. AND ALBERT A. BERG FUND IN MEMORY OF HENRY W. BERG".

I charge my Executors and Trustee hereinafter named with the duty of seeing that the conditions set forth in the papers referred to and the conditions set forth herein are duly carried out by the TRUSTEES OF THE NEW YORK PUBLIC LIBRARY.